The Very Best of 52

A poem for every week
of the year

The Very Best of 52:
A poem for every week of the year

Various Authors
Selected by Jonathan Davidson
Foreword by Jo Bell and Norman Hadley

ISBN: 978-0-9931201-7-6

52 logo © David Gillett
http://davidgillett.co.uk

First published July 2015 by:

Nine Arches Press
PO Box 6269
Rugby
CV21 9NL
United Kingdom

www.ninearchespress.com

Printed in the United Kingdom by:
Imprint Digital

The Very Best of 52

A poem for every week
of the year

Selected by Jonathan Davidson

Foreword by
Jo Bell and Norman Hadley

Nine
Arches
Press

About the Editors:

Jonathan Davidson was born in 1964 in Didcot, South Oxfordshire, and now lives in Coventry. He won an Eric Gregory award in 1990, and is the author of various pamphlets and collections of poetry, including *Moving the Stereo* (Jackson's Arm, 1993), *The Living Room* (Arc, 1994), *A Horse Called House* (Smith/Doorstop, 1997) and *Early Train* (Smith/Doorstop, 2011). His most recent publication is *Humfrey Coningsby – Poems, Complaints, Explanations and Demands for Satisfaction*. He has had eight radio plays broadcast on BBC Radio 3 and 4, along with radio adaptations of Geoffrey Hill's *Mercian Hymns* and W.S. Graham's *The Nightfishing*. His adaptation for the stage of the novel *Precious Bane* by Mary Webb for Interplay Theatre Company toured widely in 2009-10.

Jo Bell is a poet, poetry advocate and blogger whose work is widely published. Her awards include the Charles Causley Prize and a Saboteur Award for the 52 project. She ran National Poetry Day in the UK for six years and is now a freelance programmer and producer. Her poetry collection *Kith* is available from Nine Arches Press, who will publish her book of the prompts from 52 in late 2015. The 52 project is her proudest professional achievement so far.

Norman Hadley is an engine designer and mathematician who writes poetry, short fiction, children's fiction and cycling-related nonfiction to keep all the hemispheres occupied. He's produced five poetry collections so far and frenetic participation in 52 has generated sufficient material for five more.

CONTENTS

Foreword   9

1: Everything Next Year Will Be Turning, Turning   15
Robbie Burton

2: Walking to the Tube in Eight Tweets   16
Sophia Blackwell

3: Exposing Myself   17
Paul Burns

4: Invitation to Disaster   18
Clare Shaw

5: On Dolphin Poetry   20
Simon Williams

6: How Snow Comes   21
Simon Williams

7: Life's an Accumulator   22
Janice Windle

8: To Be Worn With a Black Tie   23
Graham Burchell

9: How We Settle Things Now   24
Norman Hadley

10: Touched   25
Rachel McGladdery

11: In Praise of Wensleydale   26
Julian Dobson

12: Nut   27
Matt Bright

13: Alcohol   28
Caroline Gilfillan

14: Thirty-two Lines on Loss   29
Tom Sastry

15: Search   31
Sally Evans

16: Cryptic   32
Rebecca Gethin

17: Happy International Penguin Day   33
Lindsay Macgregor

18: Appellation   34
 Rebecca Gethin

19: First Inquest   35
Julian Dobson

20: Dear Daughter   36
Bernie Cullen

21: Inside The Fig   37
Natalie Shaw

22: Fear   39
Tom Sastry

23: mrs williams leaves a note   40
Rachael Clyne

24: Carole Bromley   41
Jug (for Ros)

25: Seth Crook   42
The Street of Purple Grass

26: Tom Sastry   43
The Lingerers

27: Building Bridges   44
Liz Breslin

28: Spent   46
Jennifer McGowan

29: Good Night, Good Night You   47
Rebecca Bird

30: Liz From Next Door   48
Rachel McGladdery

31: Summer At Leckhampton With Dead Bee   49
Natalie Shaw

32: The Wishing Well   50
Tom Sastry

33: The Phone Is Ringing   52
Cath Drake

34: It Could All Have Been So Different   55
Carole Bromley

35: Seven Year Hitch   56
Sue Kindon

36: Tom Sastry   57
The Letter Does Not Say

37: Papermaker   58
Mary Gilonne

38: Angela Readman   59
Against Suicide After All

39: Norman Hadley   60
The Girl from Coire Lagan

40: Analysing Lenin's Brain   61
Julian Dobson

41: Speaking of Apples   62
Rachael Clyne

42: Whale Song   63
Catherine Ayres

43: Stripes   64
Ailsa Holland

44: TripAdvisor™ reviews for The Overlook Hotel 65
Emma Simon

45: The Young King   67
Louise Larchbourne

46: Dumped   69
Kathy Gee

47: Complicity   70
Tom Sastry

48: Surely I Can Work This Out?   72
John Lanyon

49: Nobody Quite Understands Light   73
Simon Williams

50: Phoenix   75
Charlotte Ansell

51: Giving Up The Goat   77
Stella Wulf

52: Shingle   79
Julian Dobson

Thanks   81

Acknowledgements   83

FOREWORD

On December 31st 2013, I was wondering what New Year's Resolution to make at the stroke of midnight. I was full of love for humanity, and for poets in particular. I may have been a little drunk. I must have been a little drunk. At any rate, I wanted to give something back to the literary community which nourishes me as a writer and performer. I decided that for the fifty-two weeks of 2014, I would encourage people to make their own resolution:

Write a poem a week. Start now. Keep going.

There would be two sides to the project, both online; a weekly writing prompt at fiftytwopoetry.wordpress.com and a private Facebook group, a 'safe space' in which poets at all levels could share early drafts and invite comment. It would end on New Year's Eve 2014. Fifty-two weeks, fifty-two prompts: I called it 52.

The prompts were written by me and ten guest poets, from Philip Gross to Helen Mort. Good reading is the foundation of good writing, so we embedded in each one a handful of poems by the best historical and contemporary voices: John Donne and Michael Donaghy, Ed Bok Lee and Li Po. To really make sense of the prompt, you had to read five or six world-class poems first.

Meanwhile in Facebook, the appetite grew quickly for a community where we took our writing seriously, but ourselves less so. The privilege of seeing new work emerge from dozens of poets – many, many times each day – was breathtaking. The quality of work shared was astonishing. The culture of kindness that grew up, with poets helping each other to sharpen and shape their work through critiquing, humbled us all. I roped in Norman Hadley, an innocent bystander in the 52 forum, to help with the ego-wrangling and calming of waters that sometimes prove necessary in a group of 500 poets. He became a vital second-in-command and co-editor of this book, putting in many days of work and becoming part of 52's architecture.

Thousands of poems were written in 52. Some won national or international prizes, got published in respected journals or emboldened their writers to take up postgraduate courses. The 52 project itself won a coveted Saboteur Award, and I found myself the astonished recipient of an honorary doctorate. Norman set up a donor fund for the charity Arch which raised £1000. These accolades are gratifying, but they are not the point. Poetry is a process of working out what it really is that you need to say, and finding out how best to say it. Not everyone can win a prize or get published: but everyone in 52 worked hard to write the best poetry they could, and help others to do the same. It was a triumph of kindness over ego.

This little book can't begin to represent the huge range of voices, nor the personal and literary triumphs or crises we shared. From a pool of thousands, we offer up a trickle – just one poem from each week, chosen by poet Jonathan Davidson from a shortlist with the authors' names removed. These are only nuggets from the rich seams of 52. For every person shown here, ten or twelve remain unseen. We thank them for their generous support of the 'chosen few'. (The two poems of Norman's that appear in this book came from my shortlist; like all the others, they were selected 'blind' by Jonathan.)

This is not 'community poetry' – it is a community of poets. We are proud to offer a sample of the 52 bill of fare. Read one a week, or feast on them all at once. If they whet your appetite then look out for my own book *52: Write a poem a week. Start now. Keep going,* published November 2015 by Nine Arches Press, in which all of the prompts will appear. But for now:

Read a poem a week. Start now. Keep going.

Jo Bell

I wandered into Jo's project by mistake. With an hour to kill in an airport lounge and a thin mist of WiFi to play with, I peeked in at what she was up to. It could not have been more obvious that 52 was a Force For Good if it had had "This is a Force For Good" written on it in fifty-foot letters of fire. From the start, the quality of writing, the acuity of the feedback and the warmth of the badinage were exceptional. So began a life-transforming year that instigated hundreds of deep friendships, degrees for some and a four-figure sum raised for the domestic violence charity Arch. What was it Auden said about poetry changing nothing?

As Jo says, these fifty-two poems represent a minuscule fragment of the tens of thousands posted. In addition, we've only included the poems; what you won't see in this book is the flood of incisive, kind and witty feedback that helped shape them. Neither will you see how members of the group lifted up each of these poets when their mojo had fallen into the wastepaper basket among the scrunched-up tissues. All those good folk are represented here, if you look hard enough.

Norman Hadley

This book is dedicated to the 52ers

Robbie Burton

Everything Next Year Will Be Turning, Turning

For climbers there'll be a stripping away
of chairs and toast and shampoo and wheels
until all that's left will be rock and ice and
if they're lucky
blue sky.

They'll bless each day
that begins and ends with enough thin air
to suck in.

Everyone else will scaffold their lives
with water and iPhones and oxen
and libraries and
if they're lucky
aspirin.

As far as anyone can predict
in Himalaya or hospice
supplies of thin air
won't stop.

Sophia Blackwell

Walking to the Tube in Eight Tweets

It's morning. All North London streams with cars,
distant neons twitching over Barnet.
The lift hums in its cage. The hall smells of cigars.

White headlights are like spotlights, it's still half-dark.
Two Caribbean women talk, their voices ascending,
a shock of green-tailed birds.

Here are mock-Tudor copies of Park Crescent.
Frail Pre-Raphaelite schoolgirls brandishing smartphones.
The heavy walk of disappointed women.

This new Italian restaurant has an app.
Some trophies wait for names. I watch a man stacking plums
gently as eggs, each fruit a bruised sun.

By the notice-board with its lost-looking palms,
thin girls are modelling leopard-print scarves.
A couple cross the road in a helix of arms.

A dominatrix waiting for the bus
watches a diva with a Mulberry bag spark a first fag.
Kids' scooters are carried back home by abashed dads.

Today's headlines say: *After the Verdict, More Rage.*
The sky looks half-erased and oddly static.
They say we're due another spate of winter.

Trees twenty times taller than me are swaying.
Their gentle movement looks somehow amused,
like they're whispering, *Look up once in a while.*

Paul Burns

Exposing Myself

When it comes down to it, I never considered
at the time how you saw me
I approached you on the bed and was suddenly
full of you, too full to think
and your skin tight and smooth around you
and enclosing me too, and felt my nerves rigid, exploring
how I thought you might feel about this, and how
this pulled me inside out

so much was this about you, your figure
this completion of your picture now you were naked
that I lost sight of myself, of what might be reflected
in your pale eyes; I was unclothed to the point
of not interrupting light, and so the memory of me
is blank, when I think of myself then exposed
it comes down to you

Clare Shaw

Invitation to Disaster

Come over. The storms have all cleared
and the skies now are silver.
Today is the right sort of day.
My windows are washed and the gate is unlatched.
The backyard is shiny with rain.
Come on in –

your fists full of flowers and fireworks and letters.
I've a gut full of nothing; a head full of hunger.
The key is just under the pot.
Don't dress up –
I'll know by your smell of cordite and feathers
and I'll leave all the lights full on.

Come soon.
You know how I can't stand silence and stillness.
I'm sick of the illness of sofa, TV.
Let's leave it behind us. Let's run to the forest.
Let's walk in high places in high winds and darkness;
through wastelands in cities

where strangers are waiting;
on the slick banks of rivers in spate.
Let's eat. I know what you like
and my cupboards are packed.
My heart is a handful of meat.
Bring a plate.

Bring me gifts.
Come with fire and fast water, with bright lights and thunder.
Come with your moments of grace.
You can soak all my clothes,
rest your head on my shoulder.
Bring me to tears, to my knees.

Come with a bottle.
Please.

Simon Williams

On Dolphin Poetry

"Of course our poetry is mainly oral,
although one or two experimental pieces
involving the placement of pebbles, shells
and small crustaceans have been tried
by the Language Pods, with varying success.

Before that, most work was seascapes
or about relationships. There is a school of poets
now, though, who are trying to relate
more to the world we see about us,
to inhabit the skins of other creatures.

It's hard, of course, not to be labelled
cetaceomorphic – applying dolphin characteristics
to lesser beings – but there is value, if we can
explore the way they behave, or even reason
(assuming that verb is not itself impertinence).

I heard a recitation only yesterday;
a celebrated humpback from the Southern Seas
trying to get into the mind of a human, move behind
the bizarre squeaking, the inexhaustible
desire to kill. It was thought-provoking,

but in the end, I wonder at the value in it.
Very few dealings with humans have proved helpful.
The few who have a modicum of understanding
are only interested in notation. As I said to
Chkchkchkchkchk, *a poem does not float, but flows.*"

Simon Williams

How Snow Comes

This is the light
mint white
which holds down
February's first
burst of fern.

Arrives gentle
as a mother
with a duvet
of sky-wide
smoke.

After dark,
under Scoriton's
one street lamp,
orange petals
fall.

Janice Windle

Life's an Accumulator

There's no such thing as arbitrage
in life, said the tic-tac man.
You can start as a banker but hedge your bets.
You might be a Bismarck yet.
If your sire and dam are thoroughbred
and the draw is good, you could be a jolly
but the going's hard when you start as a maiden,
in a handicap or overweight.
It's no good greening when the going's soft
even if they say you're a steamer.
There are no walkovers – we're all drifters
so don't go chasing, blinded by blinkers,
the Clerk of the Course will weigh you in
with the rest of the field at the finishing line.

Graham Burchell

To Be Worn With a Black Tie

Sell me a shirt cut from an English sky,
never quite white, nor graphite grey.
Make it extra large with seagulls, luminous
smudges, crossing a breast pocket full of rain.

Sell me a shirt where dyes bleed and darks
have faith in blue,
but being poor mimics, muster at best,
the damson of a bruise.

Sell me a shirt where no two buttons
are the same but the cuffs, sleeves and collar
sit seamless and its black label bears the words
shirt maker in silver thread.

Sell me a shirt drawn over a stiff card frame,
held with thumb-prick pins under a sheath
of cellophane, and the whole, like a gift, cradled
in a clean white box to be saved.

Norman Hadley

How We Settle Things Now

The poet, wearying of bullies, publically challenged
Vlad the Invader to combat, mano-a-mano.
Interpreters on flashing hotlines nodded frowns,
He lose, he give the other country back.
Vlad strode the arena, bare-chested though the night was freezing,
dead grass drooping from his plastic antlers.
The poet showed up, resplendent in a sequinned jockstrap
accessorised with a lamé cape which he frisbeed off,
cleared his throat and spoke,
Pawn to king four.

Rachel McGladdery

Touched

Su said you'd visited,
unsure of your new nature,
knocked a Dolly from a shelf
and it landed, plastic,
in a pose of death
right on her pillow
and she'd panted to the lamplight
I'm not scared
then felt a feather trace her cheek,
one downward stroke.

I don't know if you stretched the membrane,
pushed through with force of feeling then
but, yesterday,
in the carpet hush,
you strange in oak and satin,
my marble matryoshka with the awkward set
of those old beads concealing cuts,
I ached to lift your shoulders,
let your head fall back
and wrench those so loved blunted fingers loose
and make you look like rest
but
I was scared
and whispered of regret and love and sang
and let my eyes drop kisses where I'd like to touch.

At last I left a lip-balm smear
on your poor forehead,
and left burned by the surprise of cold.

Julian Dobson

In Praise of Wensleydale

It's a sweetness that can only rise from limestone
it's the sharpness of a certain kind of grass
it's a flying spark from horseshoe or from grindstone
the imprint of a tractor's tyres at dusk

It's a snorting Friesian's udder at the milking
the reversing of a tanker in a yard
it's water stained by soil and shot like satin
the first frost glinting in the hazel wood

It's the press and squeeze and strain of a mutation
it's the hooting of an owl along your spine
it's the block, the wire, the moment of incision
the presence and the constancy of rain

It's the parting of the liquid from the solid
the unstable balance of a dry stone wall
the cavorting of a beck in April sunlight
it is the final crumbling of it all

Matt Bright

Nut

She is always fucking, always giving birth
to gods. Who else could stand it?

She eats the sun. She points everywhere.
She is a cow. She is a pig. She is a tree.

She is a bad answer. But we were busy
with wheat and bricks. Leave us alone!

All this can't be our fault. You,
with your telescopes, could you do better?

We look up. We see her. We don't see her.
We don't look up. We see her. We don't see her.

Only the mad could worship her.
May she be praised above all others.

Caroline Gilfillan

Alcohol

He turned up in our house
with stains on his jacket and piss on his pants
and soon enough a bittery spew ran down the stairs
when he was around my brother for too long.

As for my father – he and alcohol were old muckers.
Night after night, he invited that bundle
of smarm
to paint peat in his mouth and
pump tar through his veins. I hid behind the sofa

but wouldn't you know it, the cheeky fucker
sweet-talked his way in my door
eventually

bringing his bag of not-enough, never-enough
love, not-love, things in the mouth,
family bitters,
black patent leather pumps.

These days his belly's gone to flob.

My god, though, he made my mouth wet
when he first appeared in my kitchen
in a baggy jacket
loose on the shoulders
hanging some fancy designer name off
slender shoulders. Underneath his threads ran
a pearly spine you'd want
to run your tongue down.
And I did.

Tom Sastry

Thirty-two Lines on Loss

Everywhere, they are selling:
the sun in orange juice; the sex
in perfume; thirty pence from a box
of fishfingers, tasting of sea. I lost

my glasses. I left them on the table
in the café because I was tired
of looking at billboards and wanted some thoughts
of my own and because I liked the fog of it

but when I went to leave, they were gone.
It was Sunday and the opticians
were closed. I soon realised that the world
is full of monsters travelling too fast

one of which is time. I spent a lot of time sitting that day.
I drank a lot of coffee because it is what I do
when I sit. Perhaps I drank too much. I
did a lot of thinking and I wanted it

to last longer. But the sun set
and the sun rose and I called in sick
and got some new glasses. They filmed me
in the frames. I looked like a total dick

staring straight ahead like the world's
toothiest convict. You always do.
You accept it. They said it would take an hour
to make them up, so I went out

29

into the fog and found a café. I just killed time and
checked my phone but when I went to go
I couldn't get up. My body was a sandbag.
I cried like a doll. I must have really hated the idea

of functioning again. I hated it so much.
I hated it so much that for a moment
the surprise of how much I hated it
stopped everything, even the hate.

Sally Evans

Search

This is the piece of paper I can't find.
I can't show you it, I'm sifting
through heaps on the desk, on shelves, on the floor.
It drives me crazy. I know I had it yesterday.
I always keep it safe. It is white, oblong, slim, shifting,
printed in black with some sort of header.
It's here somewhere. Yesterday
it was my MOT, Monday
it was the phone bill, Tuesday
it's a friend's poem, well, a copy of it.
Wednesday it's Tuesday, Thursday
the card I bought for my brother.
Last week it was a letter from history
and now it 's a packet of sweet pea seeds.
It could be my brain, all my memories
thrown down all over the floor,
under the bed, or in houses
I don't live in any more.
It could be people I used to love
and still do in some pigeonhole.
It could be the whole concept of love,
which turns into self preservation
or something more or less suspect,
it could be something I thought was on paper
but is actually an internet file.
Ah, I remember. I pinned it on the fridge.
I've forgotten what it said, and it's
too long ago to matter.

Rebecca Gethin

Cryptic

Sometimes I find my father and mother
walking around inside me, as if my body were their vehicle.

They look through my eyes at the hedges flashing by,
thinking thoughts, knowing mine.

I can't extricate myself from the bones I've been born into –
neither the shape of my arms in their sleeves of skin

nor my wrinkled hands on the steering wheel.
Nothing seems constant any longer.

The expression of their frozen faces is melting
 in the heat of my blood… as far as I know,

they haven't met each other for decades but they're talking
together inside my ribcage – as if I'm not here.

Lindsay Macgregor

Happy International Penguin Day

No wonder they're endangered –
it takes a certain knack to keep him
on her back for the seconds
while they mate, like balancing
one bottle on another.

Divorce is not unknown for though
the female tends to choose her partner
according to his thoughtfulness and his capacity
for raising chicks upon his feet, she'll sometimes
copulate while on her way to sea with an altogether
stronger, more aggressive-looking male.

She's memorised the outline of mountains,
moons and icebergs and navigates by breaking
waves to relocate the shore which leads to home.
But there's precious little cover on the tundra
when giant petrels swoop, intent on pecking out
the innards of the wounded and the young.

When he calls, the other birds fall silent
so she can recognise her Emperor.
They'll clean each other's feathers
as an act of adoration, quite forgetting
they've forgotten how to fly.

Rebecca Gethin

Appellation

When it was just him and me, my Dad called me 'Rah' –
He used my full name only when I'd done wrong.
To everybody else I was always 'Rebecca'
until I jettisoned her in my teens.

Nowadays if I hear someone say 'Rebecca'
it's usually someone else, not me at all.

But 'Rah' is what's written in pink letters
down through my core like a stick of rock,
blurred but unbitten. I just heard his voice
calling me back in from the garden – I won't rush.

Julian Dobson

First Inquest

It was the glowing cigarette
handed from a passenger seat
into the driver's eye
that did it.

A lads' trip: father and son,
the wet road to Sheppey.
That and the cigarette
I remember.

I noted every detail
in what was then meticulous
shorthand. The notebook
was Air Force blue.

We were instructed to draw margins
down the right side of the page
to mark what was essential.
A place to highlight details

like that cigarette. Like the comments
of the coroner, which I forget.
Or the landslide in the son's face
which still rumbles

in aftershocks in all those faces since,
crumpling in recognition
of faces they'd give anything
to recall.

Bernie Cullen

Dear Daughter

Sitting beneath a Picasso print
of a woman nursing her baby,
I'm in the room next to you,
in a Balkan coastal town, cursing
the mosquitoes that pursue me.

We have taken a trip on the glassy
sea to Our Lady of the Rocks.
We have walked through the market,
tasted olives and strawberries,
indulged in earrings.

Still you slip from me under
the duvet of stifled sobs, you say
the best that can happen
is you will never wake up.

I say, *I wish the fucking angel,*
who guided you over the Rainbow Bridge
to me, had left the fucking manual.
I'm improvising, bear with me.

Is there a reset button we haven't found yet?
Do we both dread the days ahead, staring
at the blinking lights on the foreign router,
searching for connection and steady mode?

Natalie Shaw

Inside The Fig

The flower is on the inside,
we wake in the flower our mother
became, we wake, all of us

wake. What we see
is this: our brothers have eaten
into our beds to fuck us.

We are awake. Something
outside must be got; our lovers
have made the path and light

prickles in, we push to the light
awake we fly in the bright,
our brothers sleep in a blossom

tomb but we fly. Something
calls us through the light,
it is whole it is waiting it is perfect

what is it what is it we follow
the path what is it what is it
we cannot bear it, it must

be now is it now ostiole
too small to make the path
we push with our teeth with our heads

we push off our feelers, we push off
our wings and inside the fig
we have it, out of the bright

it is perfect. Here we lay
the lovers, new ones, ready
to start again. The flower

is on the inside, we sleep
in the fruit of the flower until
we wake, all of us wake

Tom Sastry

Fear

I woke up one day and I realised how frightened I was. I was frightened of anger. I feared all anger, whatever the cause. It was all for me. It knew my name. It was waiting. There wasn't enough love in my life to ward it off. There wasn't enough love in the world to ward it off. I tanned my skin into hard leather and shrank my heart into a universe the size of a pea. Perhaps you noticed. I didn't tell you because I was afraid you would hate me too.

The next day I wasn't frightened at all. Everything was white. There was no background noise. I let all the whispers breathe into my face. They smelled of company. I took them all in and made each one sound like a bell. I was grateful for everything, even pain. I stopped telling stories. Shoal upon shoal slithered into my dead waters. New muscles governed my face. I was as busy as a hive and as lonely as a star. I felt all the colours at once. I didn't know where I was.

Rachael Clyne

mrs williams leaves a note

dear bill

you left me a note
think a plummy excuse
will save you.

ps your dinner is in the wheelbarrow

Carole Bromley

Jug
for Ros

Your garden in spring was filled with white blossom,
pale crocuses, snowdrops, narcissi
but the day before you died I ordered flowers.

My basket, because I kept pressing *order*
and nothing happened, totalled £311

so I gave up and rang them, ordered a jug,
a simple cottage garden jug of stocks,
salmon pink lisianthus, alchemilla mollis

and three Antique Duett roses. My note said
'with all my love'. The call centre girl asked

What is the occasion? Birthday or a celebration?
I didn't know how to answer.
Do you want kisses and if so how many?

I was mean with my kisses, Ros. I answered *one*.
All that morning I pictured you receiving it.

There was no reply when they knocked.
They left them in the garage.

Seth Crook

The Street of Purple Grass

bows with the wind.
The tips will reach my shoulders
when I pass.
None quite as purple
as the mass of marsh orchids,
or the sage flowers,
they sometimes look hand-dyed.

In the distance,
in the village,
at the edge of the Atlantic,
the street of fishermen
leans westward with the wind,
like fishermen bending
to kiss their slightly smaller wives.

Tom Sastry

The Lingerers

1.
We haze into the day
like the slow smell
of gorse
we jumble together
like cloth magnets.
we are offered limbs
soft gravity
clumsy elation.

2.
We're dressed and late and not sorry
the Gods are proper pissed off
they give us space missions
they give us children and paperwork.

3.
When we meet again
it's a hundred years
my body is no-one's good news
you are still beautiful
you hold back
waiting for permission
do I look that frail?
must I say
please touch me
a little further
than you would a stranger
just to show you remember.

Liz Breslin

Building Bridges

was what we did with Lego
when I was ten and you were eight and they
weren't Shell-supported movie whores
making pink shit, serious money and angry
brown men. But this is not about them.

It is not about us having sofa
hut battles: tuffleheads (your team) taking
on the bucketheads (mine). We took sides.
Always did

but there were good
NothingsGonnaStopUs KnowHerSoWell
times. The Pooh postcard you sent: promise
you'll never forget me, not even when
you're a hundred. And who will ever be
so old? Though this is not about maturity
or who has more years than who.

We were CommonPeople
in Thailand, played soccer at that orphanage
with flash Filipino smiles. I carried you, spewing,
across the Nepali border. Stories we
shared, though this is not about those

and this is not about the
Christmas Day you stood a breath away
and I handed you champagne (though it
was from Tescos not a terroir and did
not deserve its name but this is not about
the hangovers that cheap bubbles cause).
You took the glass. Turned. Flinty, daring
me to strike. But I was still building bridges
so I apologised

for what? don't ask me that, don't
make me span again the who said booh which time.
I've moved on, sister, my sorry gulf run dry.

The thing about bridges
is you can't build them from one side.

Jennifer McGowan

Spent

At 1:37 AM, we lie entwined,
not touching. We are spent,
our eyes closed, dreaming of hours
when we synchronised – when we thought
in "we" instead of "you." Now skin
is stranger to skin; our eyes
see anything but the other. So this
is how the world ends: making a wish
on the other's wishbone, breaking,
never quite letting go.

Rebecca Bird

Good Night, Good Night You

We divided the territory with a series of peace treaties:
You will snore exactly the same as before, roll and tumble
in your dreams with the turning circle of a helicopter.
And there will be no concern when I place myself entirely
inside the duvet, second-skinned in cotton, hoping
that serial killers are allergic to covers, to tight-closed eyes.
Oh I will let you whisper to God, but you must defer
to me immediately if he happens to murmur back.
I have something to discuss with him. No, it can't wait –
If the dusk should creep over the back fence
and press his hairy torso in at the window again
then the responsibility must fall to the hall light
to intervene, put up a fight. Though the shared airspace
of the blankets must be jointly patrolled;
our love cannot be revived by feet grasping
absent-mindedly in their little sleeps.

Rachel McGladdery

Liz From Next Door

I was marooned and every day an ache of misery and
grief with four kids scrapping round my ankles but
you hauled me up with kicks and curses scolding
me back we gave a little when the posh voice that
you saved for me grew see-through and I got brave
enough to rough your racist knee-jerks then it were
all in and out each other's houses and you even had
a key for nights when the oil black whiskey bog rose
up around him and he pummelled you soggy was
all 'Rach, put kettle on' and we'd sit for a 'laal 'brew
or a one-skinner when your J had green us ironing
in tandem pissed ourselves at something we found
funny starting fights in t' Rafa when you'd left your
bag at home Ah it was ace, you tiny Whitehaven
petrel raucouser than all the Fleetwood gulls – so
glad you're on my side.

Natalie Shaw

Summer at Leckhampton With Dead Bee

You have a part in a restoration
drama. You live in a little room

at the top of a flight of stairs. You stand
in the sun, rehearse and later, alone, you make

salade à l'échalote,
or au chèvre, like you learnt in France

two summers ago. The room is yours,
for the summer. In the shade, you press your hand

on an unseen bee and the itch takes over,
at night you wake to scratch and wonder

where it will stop – night follows night,
you wake and itch, you burn in the dark.

Your costume is a shiny white dress;
your breasts pop out but the director is tired

of your complaints, your part is small.
In the pool at Leckhampton you float,

look up to trace the sun in the leaves
reversed across your shut eyes

no longer a fine lady with a love
of fine china, an impossible itch,

you float in the sun, and this is your home,
this is your home, breathe it in, breathe it in.

Tom Sastry

The Wishing Well

By the time the mint-man bashed this hot disc
with his hammer
the head he struck onto it
had been severed from its fortune

leaving this coin:
a token of forbidden history
one of a small handful
a lucky penny, not kind

but full of ungoverned chance.
Last year, pressed into this girl's hot weak hand
it scared General Typhus
and his army

who dropped their dark dimpled morsel
back into its family. Worn on a string
it sleeps on her breast bone
an accidental hexagon

of greening alloy and desperate hope.
I want it.
That's why I ignore her other treasures
her tears and her prayers.

Yesterday, she threw me a straw doll
burst through with juvenile love
and asked again for her mother's health
I gave it no echo.

I coughed it into a ditch.
I want that penny and her secret desire –
the unworthy one – is hers for the asking.
She tugs at her neck. I think she knows.

Cath Drake

The Phone is Ringing

The phone is ringing inside a shell
that washes up on South Beach.
A dog yanks the shell like a piece of meat
then makes it bleed on dry sand.
The phone is ringing under the floorboards
at Edward Street which has been done up now
so there's no holes in the verandah floor.
The current tenants move about in linen suits
thinking they'll complain about the noise.
The phone is ringing inside a big dark red rose
on Curlew Road, that smells unbelievably sweet
but they're all inside, partly deaf, doors closed,
the blue TV light flashing across the windows.
The phone is ringing in the maths class
at Hollywood High. I hope it's inside
Mr Hennessey's desk drawer so it rings
in the silence after the class is told off.
But it's not, it's all housing estate now,
the ringing is far underground and I didn't
even know Mr Hennessy had cancer.
The phone is ringing in a pillow slip
in Manarola, Italy, a place we stayed on the cliff
over the azure Mediterranean in perfect weather
that you called Our Homeland. Our room
is empty tonight; a couple hear the ringing
through thin walls but it barely interrupts their love making.
The phone is ringing on an outside table
at the Aubergine Cafe, South Terrace

with the best homemade muesli in the 90s.
I'm not sure it still has that name or that muesli.
Eventually the waitress takes the phone
to lost property where it waits and waits.
These days, she says, *people leave everything*
lying about. Three friends giggle
on their way to the beach sunset.
The phone rings in the pot plant where I put
my stone collection that you laughed at,
but you're not in the garden today,
neither is your neighbour who gave you a cat.
The phone is ringing off the pier at Cottesloe,
near where a concrete water paddling pool used to be.
It's a blustery day, no one is going out
to the end of the pier today.
The phone is ringing at the Arc de Triomphe,
the volume up high but the traffic is much louder.
So many people but no one to answer it.
Under the curved arch someone calls out
to the back of a head *is that you, I don't believe it?!*
The phone is ringing at the Smith's corner shop
and the shopkeeper thinks it's kids
messing about again. No other reason
that the stack of bananas is ringing.
The phone is ringing on the next street.
I mis-dialled. I was thinking of something else.
It's ringing in a flat I hated but I did have a boyfriend
who kissed in the doorway.
The phone is ringing halfway between yours
and your parents, on a verge though
verges are big in this part of town.
The phone is ringing at Claremont Pool,
next to the sparkling Valencia Orange Drink.
It's very busy today. The attendant doesn't even

turn around; the swimmers keep lapping and lapping.
The phone is ringing at your empty parents' place.
The dog twitches, the tabby cocks its head –
both imagine dinner.
The phone is ringing at your place,
I think next to the computer, and you
pick it up but you're not very interested to talk.
You say you haven't eaten much, you can't taste
and you don't have much interest in anything.
The phone is ringing downstairs next to your car.
It keeps ringing through the night, the next few days.
It rings while you get up, drive to your parents' place,
come back, drive to your brothers, come back.
The phone is ringing, sweetheart –
it's all I have this far from home.

Carole Bromley

It Could All Have Been So Different

If I'd had just one more glass.
If I'd had one less.
If I'd got into that taxi.
If we hadn't held hands.
If we hadn't run, laughing, across the bridge.
If there'd been a bus at the stop.
If our bench had still been there.
If you hadn't led me down Black Horse Passage to the Foss.
If it hadn't been snowing.
If you hadn't taken off your warm gloves and put them on
    my hands.
If I hadn't cried.
If I hadn't asked you.
If you hadn't said yes.
If there'd been no cab.
If the street lights hadn't looked like pearls in the fog.
If there hadn't been cows.
If, with that first match, the fire hadn't taken.

Sue Kindon

Seven Year Hitch

Every seven years
we throw out the wedding photos
with the dishwater. We have been known
to smash the outsize sofa with an axe,
hastening its exit through the open door.
We leave what is precious; and stuff
the little that is left into travel bags
to fit our own backs.

We make no bones of begging a lift
without a sign board. Back seat Cabriolet
or clapped out Skoda, we jump in;
cruising neutral territory,
living rough for a while in a tangle
of woodsmoke; before we shower
and start again with a new round
of plates and another set of cutlery.

Tom Sastry

The Letter Does Not Say

what will or will not be in the fridge in six months' time;
where you will live and who you will love.

Nor does it say why. I blame the wings
of hypothetical butterflies for everything. I hold them

under my imaginary wheel. I silence all the crowing
metaphors. No dominos fall anymore.

No thing follows another. I kill the idea
of destiny by throwing so many pebbles

into the pond that no-one could say
which ripples make which storms

or which consequences
have mattered most to me.

The letter does not go this deep:
it is just the epilogue

to the story of a tree. Something happens
and you can't see what it is

because there are too many answers. But the Day After
Everything Changed, I woke in my normal bed,

oblivious to my body as always.
Then I drowned in something called the world.

Mary Gilonne

Papermaker

Water-logged with aspen, larch and fir, he takes cream pulp,
settles it down as sweet as curds, paddles a long dark
oar across and rests. A quiet surface of page shores up
along the frame and ferries his thoughts to monasteries,
a meditative marsh of birds, her wading thighs like gleaming carp.
He can almost hear a fishering of bells drifting lines across the fens,
see Ely floating, hardly moored to any land-locked thing.
Rimed, his hands hang parchment white, salted,
drying this absence of her. She has nearly gone,
only a shoal of books and bags, bones of little things are left,
her waiting shoes bask delicate as minnows. He's watermarked,
hold him to light, see how the press of her is printed through him.

Angela Readman

Against Suicide After All

I am done with you and a courtship of nights
when you slipped in with lilies, wrapped your arms

around me in a suit of grey cloth and softly
asked me to dance. I still feel your breath

sometimes, alone, a brush of suede on my neck,
but I won't be seduced. That girl is dead,

sick of the notes you leave by the bed: *Did you
ever wonder what a party's like when you're not there?*

I fell for you, of course, at sixteen, twenty one,
rolled in filthy sheets, your leg cocking mine,

unable to resist pills you wrapped in pretty bows,
simple as sweets. I've sucked your steel tongue,

broken glass in my wrist, and woke to find you gone,
a *Later* post-it left on the drawer. There are no laters

for us after all. I hang up on the dialling tone
of your voice on the line. Tell me nothing of poets,

flirt no more. Tonight I see your fist like a boxer
unsure he can win, refusing to take a fall in the fifth.

Norman Hadley

The Girl from Coire Lagan

So small, she was, so dainty,
slim-limbed as a ballerina.
We didn't know this then,
lounging by the lochan in the sun,
just listening to the tinkling scree
to see a figure coming down the Stone Shoot,
just a dot of colour in a slithering of rocks
until this pixel of humanity
was being chased, as in an arcade game,
a boulder bigger than a grand piano
rolling end-on-end, unhurriedly
towards this person who we thought,
most likely, male and butch and bearded
like it mattered, but it missed her,
like it mattered, and she made it to the bottom,
like it mattered, and she passed us, barely
flattening the grass, with bangles jangling
on wrists the width of kindling.

Julian Dobson

Analysing Lenin's Brain

Sliced deftly as prosciutto
at the Ritz, these slivers may hold genius
but I feel only sweat, blood pounding

in my temples. I have clear orders
from the Immortalisation Commission.
Examine each section,

discover signs of greatness. My heart
drums like toy soldiers, my eyes
strain under strip lights, the walls

of the Moscow Brain Institute seep
as I seek to decipher these maps:
a dry archipelago under glass.

Thirty-one thousand waterless islands:
not one means a thing to me.
I'm searching for flashmarks,

shadows of revolutionary thought,
the flush of a motherland's pride,
or even the hint of a crash

of conscience, regret at comrades
shot in the back by their friends,
lovers strangled in bed. There's only

numbness. Outside, October
is rotting. A whiff of pestilence.
The pounding of four sets of hooves.

Rachael Clyne

Speaking of Apples

When I'm in their skin
stuffed and swimming in juice
I'm very hot and sweet to eat.
A bit like Proust

I keep the doctor tempted
with knowledge of sin
as he recalls grandmother's
apple tree, her garden.

Quickly then, the scent of green,
of crisp flesh or tarte tatin,
burn of rough cider on the tongue;
a blackbird against pink, blossom, blush.

Catherine Ayres

Whale Song

I hear them in the strange dissonance of the fridge,
the hollow roar of the tumble dryer.
On windy days they scatter
high frequencies in scraps of sound,
whistle close harmonies through a half-closed gate.
I rattle with their repetitions,
a Russian doll trapped in layers of lament.
I'm going to sing back an echo.
It will rise like a moon in my throat,
spread through a staccato of doors
and disappear in a lorry's howl.
I will find silence.
A small ache of sunlight.
My shadow flickering like a fin.

Ailsa Holland

Stripes

The man with a raccoon on his shoulders
got on the tram to Piccadilly.
The raccoon looked nervous and shuffled about
and the young people were taking photos

on their phones and laughing,
not only unkindly,

and the man told us that raccoons are very social
and into everything and you can't have one

and a nice house and a few of us shared a smile
as it struck me how honest he was

making the thing that was odd about him
so visible.

Emma Simon

TripAdvisor™ reviews for The Overlook Hotel

"We didn't want to leave!" ●●●●●
Charming staff, traditional service,
Lloyd serves a generous bourbon on the rocks
and the cutlery is always spit spot polished.
It's the kind of place you settle into, end up loving.
In fact, our girls kicked up such a god-forsaken fuss
when it was time to leave, we decided to extend our visit.
TheGradyBunch

"Marvellous Views" ●●●●◎
Gloomy exterior but panoramic views across the Rockies.
Its seclusion makes this Hotel a great retreat
for yoga enthusiasts or would-be novelists –
though the white-outs aren't ideal
for those with alcohol dependency
or a tendency towards cabin fever.
Still, remaining yoga enthusiasts should note
the caretaker cooks up a sublime omelette.

"Terrible Vacation!" ●◎◎◎◎
This was my worst vacation ever. Rooms were cramped
and the geometric wallpaper that lined
the maze-like corridors had what I can only describe
as a claustrophobic leaning.
Our bathroom window jammed,
while the doors were cardboard thin,
failing to keep out the din from the 1920s ballroom
— or my husband.
WendyRabbit

The Management of The Overlook Hotel responded to
this review:
Dear Guest, Thank you for choosing our hotel
and taking time to share your comments.
We're sorry you didn't fully enjoy your stay.
We'd like to assure you steps are underway
to address the problems you experienced
with the ~~axe-wielding maniac~~ bathroom window.

"Not what I expected, unfortunately"
◉◉◎◎◎
What happened to the topiary?
TheRealSKing, Maine.

"Plumbing Problems"
◉◎◎◎◎
The hotel management needs to undertake
extensive improvements. My room – 137 –
had visible water damage from plumbing problems
in the suite above. The lifts were filthy.
The maze closed without explanation
and the mini-bar was a joke.
What colour-blind sales rep drinks red rum?
Next year I'll be booking somewhere else
for the Colorado orthodontist convention.

"Dated Decor"
◉◉◉◎◎
Man, I still have nightmares about those carpets.
StanleyK

Louise Larchbourne

The Young King

If you had not
stepped up to the moon's highlight
rose gold, still, face to me,

the car and I would not have
cracked over your new body, honey fur.

If I had not
felt the bu-bumping cracks,
your bones under the wheels, moving my spine,

I would not have
looked back.

If I had not
looked at my rear-view mirror,
then I would not have seen
your body jerking half-lit on the road.

If I had not stopped
and turned, below the just waning moon,
pulling the wheel as I could not pull time,
your spirit, back,

then I would not have seen
your mother leave the hedgerow like a snake,
in the fast everlasting dance of mothers,
to take you in her mouth
and twist you to the dark that was your home.

If your mother had not
whipped from the leaves,
mad absolute of love,
taken you in the mouth that knew your everywhere
back to the place
you briefly lived
and briefly stood out from,

then I would not have
pulled down the window as I turned,
shouted across 'I'm sorry!'
to her, the moon, and you, and to myself.

If you had not
looked so precisely, calmly, into me,
all you, glory declaring what you were,
now, I would not still feel you.

Kathy Gee

Dumped

She gives her breasts a special look,
re-checks that little lesion in the crease.
Decides to take her old computer
to the tip, removes its hard-drive heart.
It seems a shame, when it's still working,
smiles at Phil in his fluorescent tabard.
There's a lot of it about he tells her.
As she's driving to the hospital, the radio
is making cauliflower cheese.
Another white and lumpy item.

Tom Sastry

Complicity

No-one knows where the clowns went.

Perhaps they found their own country.

Perhaps they were frightened.
Look –

there's a boy in Weston-Super-Mare
who swears he saw, lined up on the mud at low tide
small piles of red wigs, braces
bellied pantaloons and oversized shoes.

The great marquees of England stand empty
and somewhere
a melancholy lion licks an abandoned red nose
whilst children hurl themselves over the guy ropes
with *look-at-me* smiles.

If they have gone, says the PM,
it was their choice
I myself am the son of clowns.
We just wanted to disperse them
to prevent them from clustering together
in ghettoes.

It's not just the politicians.
No-one says they feel guilty
there's just a sadness.

There are record downloads of classic
bike horn and ukulele tunes. New museums
are planned. The commission on nightmares
has proposed a new terror of badgers
but we all know it won't be the same.

We do our best to remember. Last night
a group of us
sniffed trick roses on the bandstand
and wiped our dripping faces
smudging our greasepaint smiles.

John Lanyon

Surely I Can Work This Out?

x is always unknown

$ax^2 + bx + c = 0$

This stuff was easy when I was 17

a ? I do admit there's something there

b ? has shown some interest

c ? is a constant in my life

frequently -1

$$x = \frac{-b \pm \sqrt{b^2 - 4ac}}{2a}$$

Simon Williams

Nobody Quite Understands Light

Some say it's particles,
some say it's waves.
In optical articles
they say it behaves

under different rules
at the very same times,
races through graticules,
shows extra lines

where by rights there'd be none.
But how can this be?
Why it's particle/wave, son,
a duality.

So, how can a wave pass
the vacuum of space,
vibrating around
with no air to displace?

It uses itself as
its medium, girl,
like rhythm in jazz,
like mother in pearl.

Light that arrives
through our telescope lenses
reflects in our eyes,
the best of our senses

and still we don't see
how it does what they say,
though we like that it does it
at the start of each day.

Charlotte Ansell

Phoenix

This is the boy who grew up believing
his mum deserved it
that her incessant bombs of crazy
drove his dad to it.
This is the boy who
fell through the cracks,
to don't care, foster homes
and contempt,
who dreamt up a suicide pact
with his sister at eight,
to drink bleach.
Whose idea of family was so skewed
he thought the Hell's Angels
were a better bet,
who at fifteen ran a man down,
knew there was no other way.
This is the boy whose
heart was charred,
always poised, always coiled,
alert, who became the man

who once burnt a crater
through what we had,
his fingers leaving a scorch of red
to choker my neck
who cracked my head off the wall
as a set of big eyes looked up
from her tea, her whimper
becoming a scream.

I am the woman
who keeps secrets like a grate
but told only the one friend
who would recognise in this
the restraint he showed.

For this is the man
who may break the stranglehold
of generations.
It's been seven years.
I may stop counting, soon.

Stella Wulf

Giving Up The Goat

Mama learned me scarper brittle edges,
trip-trap soft on clefties.

Papa learned me lean – lean in to rock,
follow, follow, follow.

Me learn nifty – sidestep cracks and rifties.
Me learn no graze bitter-bitter trampled raze,

me reach-reach high, browse ledges,
learn munch. Me grow little nubs, me grow brave,

grow life, learn give-give-bend, earn reach.
Me teach kids four-feet-fend.

Then come Gruffs – bristle me with horn,
chests out-puff, beards strokey-strokey,

blah-blah me glassy-eyed.
Blather-blather richer pasture, wide-wide opens.

Tells of green blades stropped on leathery tongue,
the sweet-suck-scent of heathery highs.

Tells how Gruff get all good things if him strong.
If him stretch, him reach-reach sky.

Me blurt – them look me slit, narrow-narrow.
'No-no,' them wags. 'No reach for Nounous,

them's broody-breeds, made to follow.
Gruffs learned me pain to marrow.

Caused me blart so hard me split sides,
spill out innards, bawl out eyes. So hard me sick-up heart.

It looked pathetic lying there, pooled in offal and hair.
I wrapped it in the tatters of my kiddy-hide,

left it to harden beside the shucked off corns of hoofs,
the dazed gaze of rolling eyes.

I grew a thicker skin, got more guts,
clearer vision. Sharpened the points of my horns.

Julian Dobson

Shingle

One year on, back to the beaches
where you walked, the cliff path
erupting with pinks, your bones grassed over.

Clouds scudded from a continent
you'd embraced at arm's length: above
the seagull vortices, deepening blue

you once sailed with the thermals.
And me, boots on, anchored
to the twice daily baptism of earth,

the roundness of its margins. Along the bay
the pull and tug, calming clatter
of a million lumps of granite. I took two,

black and oval, slashed with quartz,
perfectly caressed by years of salt:
held one, threw one back.

Many thanks are due to the following people, who generously crowdfunded this anthology and made its publication possible:

Rob Miles, David C Byrne, Robert Peett, Charlotte Ansell, Steve Harrison, Nina Lewis, Seni Senivaratne, Petra Vergunst, Amali Rodrigo, John Lanyon, Cath Blackfeather, June Palmer, Barbara Marsh, Andy Jackson, Neil Fawcett, Claire Trevien, Matthew Dunford, Elaine Taylor, Lesley Ingram, Martin Shone, Tom Sastry, Sarah Walsh, Ina Anderson, Denni Turp, Tony Walsh, Simon Williams, Eric Bones, Clive Dee, Scott Edward Anderson, Sue Millard, Andrew Bailey, Judith Taylor, Gary Carr, Fran Baillie, Steve Smart, Sharon Black, Colin Davies, Mark Hutchinson, David Clarke, Robbie Burton, Christine York, Stella Wulf, Emma Purshouse, Nicholas Whitehead, AF Harrold, Sarah Bryson, Jane Baston, Carolyn O'Connell, Eilidh Thomas, Gillian Mellor, Kate Bendelow, David Lukens, Rachel Mann, Sue Kindon, Helen Clare, Mandy Pannett, Marc Woodward, John Mackie, Peter Raynard, Abegail Morley, Sallie Tams, Julia Webb, Miki Byrne, Charlie Jordan, Emma Simon, Mandy McDonald, Anne Marie Dagostino, Ailsa Holland, Alwyn Marriage, Char March, David Nicholson, Knotbrook Taylor, Sue Barnard, Naomi Crosby, Elaine Christie, Myfanwy Fox, Bernard Briggs, Shirley Wright, Sarah L Dixon, David Mack, Mavis Moog, Christo Heyworth, Dorothy Baird, Jeff Price, Stephanie Arsoska, Janice Windle, Marily Francis, Meg Cox, Lucy Jeynes, Matthew West, Kate Feld, Hannah Linden, Ben Banyard, Haworth Hodgkinson, Babs Knightley Short, Fiona Russell Dodwell, Marilyn Hammick, Nicky Phillips,

Bare Fiction, Max Wallis, Maureen Cullen, Kathryn Whitehead, Daniel Hooks, Jenny Hill, Julie Bird, Renita Boyle, Kate Fox, Tania Hershman, Ann Follows, Ruth Stacey, Bob Hill, Sharon Larkin, Sandra Gordon, Kevin Reid, Sally Evans, Becky Gethin, Hilary Robinson, Faye Godfrey, Roz Goddard, Carole Bromley, Nina Simon, Jessica Wortley, Trish Traynor, Dru Marland, Mildred Beere, Sarah Watkinson, Julian Dobson, Rayya Ghul, Kymm Coveney, Chris Hemingway, Lindsay Waller Wilkinson, Beth McDonough, Clare Hepworth Wain, Gram Joel Davies, Jackie Biggs, Holly Magill, Brett Evans, Angela Readman, William Gallagher, Jean Atkin, Sarah Maitland Parks, Lesley Quayle, Helen Cadbury, Maggie Mackay, Liz Williamson, Kathy Gee, Jennifer Taylor, Nell Nelson, Bernie Cullen, John and Liz Mills, Michael Mackian, Selkirk Ayres, John Michael Alwyine-Mosely, Tom Freshwater, Reuben Woolley, Mary Gilonne, Rachael Clyne, Josephine Corcoran, Roisin Bourne Hill, Ruth Aylett, Zelda Chappell, Jane Burn, Natalie Baron, Lindsay MacGregor, Angi Holden, Norman Hadley, Susan Castillo, Marjorie Nielson, Liz England, Clare Bold, Jinny Fisher, Judi Sutherland, Raine Voss, Colin Will, Cathy Dreyer, Frances Passmore, Lesley Reid, Phil Ward, Fran Wilde, Mark Gamble, Kriss Nichol, Pauline Sewards, C Edwards, Julie Sorrell, Joanne Key, Jayne Stanton, Sue Sims, Arwen Webb, Big Mamma Frog, Michael Brewer, Jamie Summerfield, Peter Doyle, Peter Richards, Jessica Davies, Margaret Walker, Martin Whatmuff, Brenda Read-Brown, JA Mcgowan, GH Turner.

ACKNOWLEDGEMENTS

Catherine Ayres' poem 'Whale Song' was published in Issue 12 of *The Black Light Engine Room*; in Natalie Shaw's 'Summer at Leckhampton with dead bee' the lines 'fine lady with a love/of fine china' are a reference to *The Country Wife*, by William Wycherley; Liz Breslin's 'Building Bridges' quotes song titles including 'Nothing's Gonna Stop Us Now' by Starship and 'Common People' by Pulp. "I Know Her So Well" is a misquote of the Tim Rice, Benny Andersson and Björn Ulvaeus song, "Promise/ you'll never forget me, not even when /you're a hundred" paraphrases A. A. Milne; Rachael Clyne's 'mrs williams leaves a note' is of course a response to 'This is Just to Say' by William Carlos Williams; Mary Gilonne's poem 'Papermaker' won the Wenlock International Poetry Competition in 2015; Julian Dobson's 'In Praise of Wensleydale' was published on Yorkmix.com April 2015 and 'Analysing Lenin's Brain' was inspired by an article by Andrew Higgins in *The Independent* on 1 November 1993; Sally Evans' 'Search' first appeared on blog *The Stare's Nest*; Simon Williams' poem 'On Dolphin Poetry' references Archibald McLeish's 'Ars Poetica'.

Jo says: Deep thanks to Norman Hadley, an ordinary member of 52 when he offered to 'babysit' 52 for a week, and thereafter an invaluable support and co-worker. Without him I could never have coped. Getting to know him better has been one of 52's great rewards. Thanks too to Jonathan Davidson, fine poet and impartial editor of this selection; and to Jane Commane of Nine Arches for typesetting and publishing. Most of all, thanks to every single member of 52. To the avid ones who took part 52 weeks in a row, and the occasional contributors; to all who selflessly helped others to refine their work; to all who threw themselves into the experiment, and also to the Lurkers who sat quietly in the shadows, reading and learning – thanks to you all. The 52 project taught me much about poets and human nature. You have changed my life; it has been a privilege.

Norman says: My thanks go to Jo for devising this extraordinary literary/social experiment, Jonathan for his final judiciousness and all the poets who joined us on this wildest of rides. I also thank my beloved, Deb, for indulging all those hundreds of reveries throughout the year, often at the most inopportune moments.